SIXTY-MINUTE SHAKESPEARE

THE TEMPEST

by Cass Foster

SIXTY-MINUTE SHAKESPEARE

THE TEMPEST

by Cass Foster

A romantic comedy (written 1611) considered to
be the last play Shakespeare wrote alone.

from THE TEMPEST
by WILLIAM SHAKESPEARE

FIVE STAR
PUBLICATIONS
Shining Brightly Since 1985

Chandler, Arizona

Linda F. Radke, President
Five Star Publications, Inc.
PO Box 6698
Chandler, AZ 85246-6698
480-940-8182
www.FiveStarPublications.com

For performance rights please contact:
Dramatic Publishing
www.DramaticPublishing.com
(800) 448-7469
www.GetShakespeare.com

Publisher's Cataloging-In-Publication Data
Names: Shakespeare, William, 1564-1616. | Foster, Cass, 1948- abridger.
Title: The tempest / [abridged] by Cass Foster ; from The tempest by William Shakespeare.
Description: Chandler, Arizona : Five Star Publications, [2016] | Sixty-minute Shakespeare | Interest age level: 11 and up. | Summary: An abridged version of Shakespeare's story about family, treachery, and love, that revolves around a father's magical manipulations to control his daughter's romantic fate and exact revenge upon his enemies.
Identifiers: LCCN 2016931120 | ISBN 978-1-58985-236-5 (print) | ISBN 978-1-58985-237-2 (ebook)
Subjects: LCSH: Political refugees--Juvenile drama. | Fathers and daughters--Juvenile drama. | Shipwreck victims--Juvenile drama. | Magicians--Juvenile drama. | Tragicomedy. CYAC: Political refugees--Drama. | Fathers and daughters--Drama. | Shipwreck victims--Drama. | Magicians--Drama.
Classification: LCC PR2833 .A25 2016 (print) | LCC PR2833 (ebook) | DDC 822.3/3--dc23

Electronic edition provided by

The eBook Division of Five Star Publications, Inc.

Printed in the United States of America

COVER DESIGN: Kris Taft Miller
PAGE LAYOUT: Renana Typesetting
COPY EDITOR: Cristy Bertini
PROOFREADER: Ruthann Raitter
PROJECT MANAGER: Patti Crane

Dedicated

TO

Kat Scarbo

Our most beautiful and valiant daughter.
Who along with your loving husband, Michael,
Brought the remarkable Addie and Finn into our world.
You struggle so fearlessly and heroically against your "tempest."
Nellie and I love you more than we could possibly put into words.

"When we fall asleep at the end of the day
Imagine we are a leaf gently floating onto the lap of G-d."

WELCOME TO
THE SIXTY-MINUTE SHAKESPEARE

No playwright, past or present, approaches the brilliance and magnitude of William Shakespeare. What other works are read more often than the Bible – and worldwide?

As one of the wealthiest people of his time, Shakespeare earned his living as a playwright, theatre manager, actor, and shareholder in the Globe Theatre. He rebelled against the contemporary theatrical standards (the neo-classical principles that limited dramatic structure throughout France and Italy), took plots from other published works (making them uniquely his own), and created a spectacle (without the use of elaborate scenery) to captivate audiences of all social levels.

Imagine the challenge in quieting a crowd of three thousand in a theatre where vendors sell wine, beer, ale, nuts, and playing cards; where there is no intermission; where birds fly overhead; and where audience members stand near performers. Such was the setting in Shakespeare's day.

The purpose behind this series is to reduce (not contemporize) the language. The unabridged Shakespeare simply isn't practical in all situations. Not all educators or directors have the luxury of time or finances to explore the entire text. This is not intended to be a substitute for a thorough study of Shakespeare. It is merely a stepping-stone.

We hope you are pleased with our series and may each of you be blessed with an abundance of prosperity, good health, and happiness.

May the Verse Be With You!

STAGING CONSIDERATIONS

SCENERY

Shakespeare staging typically contains an "upper above" (balcony) and an "inner below" (stage floor). They permit the use of different levels and locations for actors to enter and exit. If this isn't an option, consider a few small-sized classroom-acting boxes to add levels for standing and sitting. In *The Tempest,* for example, they would be helpful for Ariel, unseen by everyone but Prospero, to be in the midst of or behind the action. Adding levels will provide numerous options for blocking.

As for actual scenery, there are two excellent reasons theatres rarely use much when staging Shakespeare. The first is related to the number of changes required. If the audience has to wait every five minutes to watch scenery struck and set up, the audience ends up watching a play about moving lumber. The second is because the audience will lose sight of what the play is about. Audiences need a minute to adjust to the scenic look of a dazzling waterfall or lush forest. By the time they take it all in and start paying attention to the dialogue, it's time to set up the next scene and the audience will be lost.

Location is typically established through dialogue and the use of a few simple props: a throne-like chair for the king's court, a long table with benches for an inn, a bed for the queen's bed chamber, etc. The key is to keep it simple.

PACING

Keep things moving! That doesn't mean actors should talk and move quickly; it simply means one scene should flow smoothly to the next without delay or interruption.

As Scene 1 ends, the actors pick up their props and walk off stage right. Actors for Scene 2 enter from stage left with their props and begin dialogue as they enter the acting area, putting their props in place as they speak. You may have a view of the actors exiting from the first scene as actors enter in the second scene, but audiences will gladly accept this convention if it means taking fifteen minutes off performance time.

Line delivery: Let's say one page in your script has ten different cues. If actors take three seconds before coming in with their line, they will add thirty seconds *per page*. Ninety pages means, yep, forty-five minutes where nothing is being said. Actors will often say, "But I need time to listen and formulate my response." Yes, in real life, but not in the theatre where we are typically "lifelike." Poor pacing will result in a bored and restless audience.

Unless indicated otherwise, actors should take less than a second to come in with their lines. Work on pacing *after* they are solidly off book and remind them this is about picking up cues, *not* about speeding their delivery. Trust me, audience members will praise the pace.

SAMPLING OF SHAKESPEARE'S
IMAGES AND THEMES

Abandonment

Abusive Relationships

Allure of ruling a colony/
country

Ambition

Animals

Anti-Semitism

Astrological influence

Betrayal

Black or white magic

Bravery

Changing identities

Character

Characters reforming

Charity

Conspiracy

Corrupt society

Courage

Darkness and light

Deception

Destiny or fate

Disease or physical decay

Distinguishing men from
monsters

False accusations

Fantasy

Fertility suppression

Foils or opposites

Forgiveness

Freedom

Greed and Corruption

Heavenly retribution

Honor

Human frailty

Hypocrisy

Impact of money

Impetuous love

Insanity

Irresponsible power

Justice

Loneliness or isolation

Loss of one's soul

Love of individuals/money/
power

Loyalty

Madness

Marriage

Maturity

Melancholy

Mistaken identity

Mortality

Multiple meanings of words

Nature

Old age

Paranoia

Play-acting

Power of evil

Power/Control

Preparing for leadership

Pride

Prophecies

Real or pretended madness

Reality vs. illusion
Rebellion
Regicide
Religious persecution
Revenge
Role of women
Savagery
Seduction
Self-destruction
Self-righteousness
Sexual misadventure
Spying
Suicide

Supernatural
Temptation
The elements
The supernatural
Thought vs. action
Types of love
Tyranny
Usurping of power
Violence
War
Wisdom of fools
Witchcraft

THE COMPLETE WORKS
OF WILLIAM SHAKESPEARE

1589–1591	*Henry VI, Part 1, 2 & 3*
1592–1593	*Richard III*
1593–1594	*Titus Andronicus*
1592–1594	*The Comedy of Errors*
1593–1594	*Taming of the Shrew*
1594	*The Two Gentlemen of Verona*
1594–1595	*Love's Labour's Lost*
1594–1596	*King John*
1595	*Richard II*
1595–1596	*A Midsummer Night's Dream*
1595–1596	*Romeo and Juliet*
1596–1597	*The Merchant of Venice*
1597	*The Merry Wives of Windsor*
1597–1598	*Henry IV, Parts 1 & 2*
1598–1599	*Much Ado About Nothing*
1599	*Henry V*
1599	*Julius Caesar*
1599	*As You Like It*
1600–1601	*Hamlet*
1601–1602	*Twelfth Night*
1601–1602	*Troilus and Cressida*
1602–1603	*All's Well That Ends Well*
1604	*Measure for Measure*
1604	*Othello*
1605	*The Tragedy of King Lear*
1606	*Macbeth*
1606–1607	*Antony and Cleopatra*
1607–1608	*Timon of Athens*
1607–1608	*Pericles, Prince of Tyre*
1607–1608	*Coriolanus*
1609–1610	*Cymbeline*
1609–1610	*The Winter's Tale*
1611	*The Tempest*
1612- 1613	*Henry VIII* (Possibly co-authored)
1613	*Two Noble Kinsmen* (Authorship in question)

A FEW WORDS ABOUT SHAKESPEARE

"A remarkable thing about Shakespeare is that he is really very good in spite of all the people who say he is very good."
                                    – Robert Graves 1895–1985

"It's what Shakespeare's mission was – to illuminate our thoughts and struggles and bring about the possibility of getting the most we can out of a day as opposed to least in this brief moment we're here."
                                    – Mandy Patinkin, 1952–present

"Thank G-d* we don't know a lot about Shakespeare or Moses or Homer or Lautreamont. These are the best guys we got, and their art is powerful because they're mysterious."
                                    – Cass McCombs, 1977–present

"The records – what little we know about Shakespeare, including the records of the plays in his playhouse – were often the story of how quickly they came off if they didn't work. They had to move on. They were absolutely led by box office."
                                    – Kenneth Branagh, 1960–present

"Brush Up Your Shakespeare."
                                    – Cole Porter, 1891–1964

"Shakespeare – the nearest thing in incarnation to the eye of G-d."
                                    – Laurence Olivier, 1907–1989

"If Shakespeare required a word and had not met it in civilized discourse, he unhesitatingly made it up."
                                    – Anthony Burgess, 1917–1993

"But my G-d, how beautiful Shakespeare is, who else is as mysterious as he is; his language and method are like a brush trembling with excitement and ecstasy. But one must learn to read, just as one must learn to see and learn to live."
                                    – Vincent van Gogh, 1853–1890

*G-d: According to Professor Foster's religious beliefs, to fully write out the name of the Supreme Being turns the text into a sacred document. And that requires all copies to be handled and treated as such. So out of respect for his beliefs, we will hyphenate all usage.

23 April 1564–23 April 1616

"If we wish to know the force of human genius, we should read Shakespeare. If we wish to see the insignificance of human learning, we may study his commentators."

– William Hazlitt (1778–1830) English Essayist

COMMON QUOTES FROM THE BARD

Romeo and Juliet

"Parting is such sweet sorrow."
"A plague o' both your houses."
"O Romeo, Romeo! Wherefore art thou Romeo?"

A Midsummer Night's Dream

"Lord, what fools these mortals be."
"The course of true love never did run smooth."
"To say the truth, reason and love keep little company together nowadays."

As You Like It

"All the world's a stage"
"And all the men and women merely players."
"Forever and a day."

Twelfth Night

"Some are born great, some achieve greatness, and some have greatness thrust upon them."
"Out of the jaws of death."
"O, had I but followed the arts!"
"Many a good hanging prevents a bad marriage."

Henry IV, Part 1

"The better part of valor is discretion."
"He will give the devil his due."

Henry VI, Part 2

"Let's kill all the lawyers."
"He hath eaten me out of house and home."

The Merry Wives of Windsor

"Better three hours too soon than a minute too late."

The Merchant of Venice

"The devil can cite Scripture for his purpose."
"All that glisters is not gold."
"Love is blind."

Macbeth

"Out, damned spot. Out, I say!"
"Screw your courage to the sticking place."

Hamlet

"Something is rotten in the state of Denmark."
"To be or not to be. That is the question."
"The lady doth protest too much, methinks."
"Good night, sweet prince, And flights of
angels sing thee to thy rest!"

Pericles

"Few love to hear the sins they love to act."

Richard III

"Now is the winter of our discontent."
"Off with his head!"
"A horse! A horse! My kingdom for a horse."

Julius Caesar

"Beware the ides of March."
"Friends, Romans, countrymen, lend me your ears."
"It was Greek to me."

Much Ado About Nothing

"The world must be peopled. When I said I would die a
bachelor, I did not think I should live till I were married."

Measure for Measure

"The miserable have no other medicine. But only hope."

Troilus and Cressida

"To fear the worst oft cures the worse."

The Comedy of Errors

"Unquiet meals make ill digestions."

The Tempest

"Good wombs have borne bad sons."
"A pox o' your throat, you bawling, blasphemous,
incharitable dog!"

Casablanca

"This could be the start of a beautiful friendship."

CAST OF CHARACTERS

PROSPERO – Rightful Duke of Milan in exile

MIRANDA – His only daughter

ANTONIO – His younger brother

GONZALO – His old counselor

ARIEL – Airy Spirit – source of Prospero's magical powers

CALIBAN – Prospero's savage and deformed slave

ALONSO – King of Naples

SEBASTIAN – His brother

FERDINAND – His son

TRINCULO – His jester

STEPHANO – His drunken butler

ADRIAN – lord

FRANCISCO – lord

MASTER OF THE SHIP

BOATSWAIN – In charge of the deck crew

MARINER(S)

IRIS – spirits who may help with costume/scene changes

JUNO – spirits who may help with costume/scene changes

CERES – a spirit played by Ariel

ADDITIONAL SPIRITS or NYMPHS – if possible to add to spectacle

If you have a limited number of actors, just make
necessary text changes by eliminating Adrian,
Francisco, Master and/or Mariner(s).

DOUBLE CASTING OPTIONS
Master of the Ship / Adrian
Boatswain / Francisco
Mariner / Stephano

BLOCKING / STAGE DIRECTIONS

Some directors follow stage directions religiously, yet not all play-wrights use many, if any, stage directions. Shakespeare is an example of a playwright who relies solely on the text. Edward Albee's *Who's Afraid of Virginia Woolf?* is an example of where you will find stage directions on practically every page of the script.

Stage directions are often a depiction of how the play was staged when it was turned over to the publisher (to be used for printing). They are rarely intended for future directors to follow. There are numerous reasons playwrights provide or don't provide stage directions but let's save that for another day.

I have not blocked the entire script, but provided movement patterns in certain scenes. Some of you are experienced directors in need of little if any help with blocking and some are novices who would appre-ciate some suggestions. And that's all these are: *suggestions* – not how the show should be staged. It was my custom to provide my directing students with five different film versions of the Hamlet/Laertes fight scene to demonstrate there is no correct way to stage a fight – or a play.

Ignore the blocking or use what works. What is provided is intended to assist, not confuse or offend. This may extend beyond the sixty min-utes depending on how much business or movement you incorporate.

ACT I, SCENE 1
A SHIP AT SEA.

Sounds of rain, thunder and lightning as the MASTER *enters (as with* ALL *who enter) struggling to keep his footing on the windswept ship.*

MASTER   Boatswain!

Enter BOATSWAIN.

BOATSWAIN   Here, master. What cheer?

MASTER   Good, speak to th' mariners! Fall to 't yarely,* or we run
    ourselves aground. Bestir, bestir.

Exit MASTER.

BOATSWAIN   Heigh, my hearts! Cheerly, cheerly, my
    hearts! Yare! Yare! Take in the topsail! Blow till thou*
    burst thy wind, if room enough!

Enter ALONSO *(wearing the crown he'll wear throughout),* SEBASTIAN,
ANTONIO, FERDINAND *and* GONZALO.

ALONSO   Good Boatswain, have care. Where's the master? Play* the
    men.

BOATSWAIN   I pray now, keep below.

ANTONIO   Where is the master, bos'n?

BOATSWAIN   Do you not hear him? You mar our labor.
    Keep your cabins; you do assist the storm.

GONZALO   Nay, good, be patient.
    Remember whom thou hast aboard.

BOATSWAIN   None that I more love than myself. Give thanks
    you have lived so long, and make yourself

yarely: briskly blow   **till thou:** addressing the storm   **play:** urge

ready in your cabin for the mischance of the hour,
if it so hap. Cheerly, good hearts!
Out of our way, I say.

GONZALO (*Losing his balance.*) I' have great comfort from this fellow.
Stand fast, good Fate, to his hanging! Make the rope
of his destiny our cable, for our own doth little advantage.
If he be not born to be hanged, our case is miserable.

ALL *but* BOATSWAIN *exit.*

BOATSWAIN (*Speaking to the crew off stage.*)
Down with the topmast! Yare! Lower,
lower! Bring her to try with main course.
(*A cry off stage.*) A plague upon this howling! They are
louder than the weather* or our office.

Enter SEBASTIAN, ANTONIO *and* GONZALO.

BOATSWAIN Yet again? What do you hear? Shall we give o'er*
and drown? Have you a mind to sink?

SEBASTIAN A pox* o' your throat, you bawling, blasphemous, incharitable dog!

BOATSWAIN Work you, then.

ANTONIO Hang, cur! Hang you whoreson, insolent noisemaker!
We are less afraid to be drowned than thou art.

GONZALO I'll warrant him* for drowning, though the
ship were no stronger than a nutshell and as leaky
as an unstanched* wench.

---

louder than the weather: making more noise then the tempest   **give o'er:** give
up   **pox:** plague   **warrant him:** guarantee him   **unstaunched:** wide open

BOATSWAIN Lay her ahold, ahold! Set her two
    courses! Off to sea again! Lay her off!*

Enter MARINER, soaking wet.

MARINER All lost! To prayers, to prayers. All lost!

Exit MARINER.

GONZALO The King and Prince at prayers! Let's assist them,
    for our case is as theirs.

SEBASTIAN I am out of patience.

ANTONIO We are merely* cheated of our lives by drunkards.

GONZALO He'll be hanged yet,
    though every drop of water swear against it
    and gape at wid'st to glut him.

*Frightening cries from off stage: "Mercy on us" ... "We split. We
split." ... "Farewell my wife and children." ... "Farewell brother." ... "We
split. We split."*

Exit BOATSWAIN as the others continue swaying from the tempest.

ANTONIO Let's all sink wi' th' king.

SEBASTIAN Let's take leave of him.

Exit ANTONIO and SEBASTIAN.

GONZALO Now would I give a thousand furlongs of
    sea for an acre of barren ground – long heath,*
    brown furze, anything. The wills above be done,
    But I would fain* die a dry death.

Exit GONZALO.

lay her off: also set a course back to sea **merely:** completely **heath:** heather
grows in barren soil **fain:** gladly

ACT I, SCENE 2
IN FRONT OF PROSPERO'S CELL.

Enter PROSPERO *(with his magical staff he carries throughout) and* MIRANDA.

MIRANDA   O, I have suffered
 With those that I saw suffer! A brave* vessel
 (Who had, no doubt, some noble creature in her)
 Dashed all to pieces! O, the cry did knock
 Against my very heart! Poor souls, they perished.

PROSPERO   Be collected.
 No more amazement.* Tell your piteous heart
 There's no harm done.

MIRANDA   O, woe the day!

PROSPERO   No harm.
 I have done nothing but in care of thee.
 Of thee my dear one, thee my daughter, who
 Art ignorant of what thou art, naught knowing
 Of whence I am, nor that I am more better
 Than Prospero, and thy no greater father.

MIRANDA   More to know did never meddle* with
 my thoughts.

PROSPERO   'Tis time I should inform thee
 farther. Lend thy hand And pluck my magic garment from
 me.

She removes his cloak as he indicates where to place it.

PROSPERO   So.
 Lie there, my art. Wipe thou thine eyes; have comfort.

brave: fine **amazement:** terror **meddle:** mingle

4

For thou must now know farther.

MIRANDA You have often
    Begun to tell me what I am; but stopped
    And left me to a bootless inquisition,
    Concluding, "Stay; Not yet."

He moves a box and sits next to her.

(See STAGING CONSIDERATIONS *provided earlier in the script.)*

PROSPERO The hour's now come;
    The very minute bids thee ope thine ear.
    Obey, and be attentive. (*She sits or kneels next to him.*)
    Canst thou remember
    A time before we came unto this cell?
    I do not think thou canst, for then thou wast not
    Out* three years old.

MIRANDA Certainly, sir, I can.

PROSPERO Twelve year since, Miranda, twelve year since,
    Thy father was Duke of Milan* and
    A prince of power.

MIRANDA Sir, are not you my father?

PROSPERO Thy mother was a piece* of virtue and
    She said thou wast my daughter; and thy father
    Was Duke of Milan; and his only heir
    And princess, no worse issued.*

MIRANDA (*She rises.*) O the heavens!
    What foul play had we came from thence?
    Or blessèd was't we did?

out: barely **Milan:** pronounced Millen **piece:** masterpiece **no worse issued:**
no less noble in birth

PROSPERO Both, both, my girl!
>   By foul play, as thou say'st, were we heaved thence,
>   But blessedly holp* hither.

MIRANDA O, my heart bleeds
>   To think o' th' teen that I have turned you to.*
>   Which is from my remembrance! Please you,
>   farther.

PROSPERO My brother and thy uncle, called Antonio –
>   I pray thee mark me (*She sits.*) – that a brother should
>   Be so perfidious! – Of all the world I loved,
>   And to him put the manage of my state.*
>   The government I cast upon my brother
>   And to my state grew stranger, being transported
>   And rapt in secret studies. Thy false uncle –
>   Dost thou attend me?

MIRANDA Sir, most heedfully.

PROSPERO Being once perfected* how to grant suits,
>   How to deny them, who t'advance and who
>   To trash for overtopping,* new created
>   The creatures that were mine, I say, – or changed 'em,
>   Or else new-formed 'em – having both the key
>   Of officer and office,* set all hearts i' th' state
>   To what tune pleased his ear, that now he was
>   The ivy which had hid my princely trunk
>   And sucked my verdure out on't. Thou attend'st not.

MIRANDA O, good sir, I do.

PROSPERO (*He rises.*) I pray thee, mark me.

---

holp: helped **turned you to:** caused you to remember **state:** domain **perfected:**
expert in **overtopping:** restrain from becoming too powerful **officer and office:**
the key to power and (as in playing music) a tuning key

6

I thus neglecting worldly ends, all dedicated
To closeness* and the bettering of my mind
With that which, but by being so retired,
O'erprized* all popular rate, in my false brother
Awaked an evil nature, and my trust,
Like a good parent,* did beget of him
A falsehood in its contrary as great
As my trust was, which had indeed no limit,
A confidence sans* bound. He being thus lorded,
Hence his ambition growing –
Dost thou hear?

MIRANDA   Your tale, sir, would cure deafness.

PROSPERO   To have no screen between this part he played.
And him he played it for, he needs will be
Absolute Milan.* Me (poor man) my library
Was dukedom large enough. Of temporal royalties
He thinks me now incapable; confederates
(So dry* he was for sway) wi' th' King of Naples
To give him annual tribute, do him homage,
Subject his coronet to his crown, and bend
The dukedom, yet unbowed (alas, poor Milan!)
To most ignoble stooping.

MIRANDA   (*She rises.*) O the heavens!

PROSPERO   Mark his condition,* and th' event;* then tell me
If this might be a brother.

MIRANDA   I should sin

---

to closeness: seclusion   **o'erprized:** greater worth than any evaluation   **good
parent:** proverbial concept of a good parent bringing a bad child into the world
sans: without   **Absolute Milan:** the true Duke of Milan   **dry:** thirsty   **mark
his condition:** terms of my pact with Naples   **event:** outcome

To think but nobly of my grandmother.
Good wombs have borne bad sons.

PROSPERO Now the condition.
　　This King of Naples, being an enemy
　　To me inveterate, hearkens my brother's suit;
　　Which was that he, in lieu o' th' premises*
　　Of homage and I know not how much tribute,
　　Should presently extirpate* me and mine
　　Out of the dukedom and confer fair Milan,
　　With all the honors, on my brother.

MIRANDA Alack, for pity!
　　I, not rememb'ring how I cried out then,
　　Will cry it o'er again. It is a hint*
　　That wrings mine eyes to 't.

PROSPERO Hear a little further,
　　And then I'll bring thee to the present business
　　Which now's upon's; without the which this story
　　Were most impertinent.*

MIRANDA Wherefore did they not
　　That hour destroy us?

PROSPERO (*He sits.*) My tale provokes that question.
　　In few,* they hurried us aboard a bark;
　　Bore us some leagues to sea, where they prepared
　　A rotten carcass of a butt,* not rigged,
　　Nor tackle, sail, nor mast; the very rats
　　Instinctively had quit it. There they hoist us
　　To cry to th' sea that roared to us; to sigh

---

premises: guarantees　**presently extirpate:** immediately remove　**a hint:** an occasion　**impertinent:** irrelevant　**in few:** in few words　**butt:** tub

To th' winds, whose pity, sighing back again,
Did us but loving wrong.

MIRANDA Alack, what trouble
Was I then to you!

PROSPERO O, a cherubin*
Thou wast that did preserve me! Thou didst smile,
Infused with a fortitude from heaven.

MIRANDA How came we ashore?

PROSPERO By providence divine.
Some food we had, and some fresh water, that
A noble Neapolitan, Gonzalo,
Out of his charity, who being then appointed
Master of this design, did give us.
Knowing I loved my books, he furnished me
From mine own library with volumes that
I prize above my dukedom.

MIRANDA Would I might
But ever see that man!

PROSPERO (*Rises and puts on his cloak*) Now I arise.
Sit still, and hear the last of our sea sorrow.
Here in this island we arrived; and here
Have I, thy schoolmaster, made thee more profit
Than other princess' can, that have more time
For vainer hours, and tutors not so careful.

MIRANDA Heavens thank you for 't! And now I pray you, sir –
For still 'tis beating in my mind – your reason
For raising this sea storm?

PROSPERO Know thus far forth:

cherubin: celestial being

By accident most strange, bountiful Fortune
(Now my dear lady) hath mine enemies
Brought to this shore; And by my prescience
I find my zenith* doth depend upon
A most auspicious star, whose influence
If now I court not, but omit,* my fortunes
Will ever after droop. Here cease more questions.
Thou art inclined to sleep. 'Tis a good dullness
And give it way.

PROSPERO *weaves a spell over* MIRANDA *and she falls asleep.*

PROSPERO   Come away,* servant, come! I am ready now.
Approach, my Ariel! Come!

Enter ARIEL.

ARIEL   All hail, great master! Grave sir, hail! I come
To answer thy best pleasure, be't to fly
To swim, to dive into the fire, to ride
On the curled clouds. To they strong bidding, task
Ariel and all his quality.*

PROSPERO   Hast thou, spirit,
Performed to point* the tempest that I bade thee?

ARIEL   To every article.
I boarded the King's ship. Now on the beak*
Now in the waist,* the deck,* in every cabin,
I flamed amazement.* O' th' dreadful thunderclaps.

PROSPERO   My brave spirit!

---

zenith: height of fortune   **omit:** neglect   **come away:** come from where you are
quality: cohorts   **to point:** to every detail   **beak:** prow   **waist:** middle of the ship
deck: roof of the stern   **amazement:** struck terror by appearing as St. Elmo's fire

Who was so firm, so constant, that this coil*
Would not infect his reason?

ARIEL Not a soul
But felt a fever of the mad and played
Some tricks of desperation. All but mariners
Plunged in the foaming brine and quit the vessel,
Then all afire with me. The King's son, Ferdinand,
With hair up-staring* (then like reeds, not hair),
Was the first man that leapt; cried "Hell is empty
And all the devils are here!"

PROSPERO Why, that's my spirit!
But was not this nigh shore?

ARIEL Close by, my master.

PROSPERO But are they, Ariel, safe?

ARIEL Not a hair perished.
On their sustaining* garments not a blemish,
But fresher than before; and as thou bad'st me,
In troops I have disbursed them 'bout the isle.
The King's son have I landed by himself,
Whom I left cooling of the air with sighs
In an odd angle of the isle, and sitting,
His arms in this sad knot. (*He illustrates.*)

PROSPERO (*He sits.*) Of the King's ship,
The mariners, say how thou hast disposed,
And all the rest o' th' fleet.

ARIEL (*Sits on the ground*) Safely in harbor
Is the King's ship; in the deep nook where once
Thou calld'st me up at midnight to fetch dew

---

coil: uproar   **up-staring:** standing on end   **sustaining:** supporting

11

From the still-vexed Bermoothes,* there she's hid;
And are upon the Mediterranean float*
Bound sadly home for Naples,
Supposing that they saw the king's ship wracked
And his great person perish.

PROSPERO Ariel, thy charge
Exactly is performed; But there's more work.

ARIEL (*Rises*) Is there more toil? Since thou dost give me pains,*
Let me remember* thee what thou hast promised,
Which is not yet performed me.

PROSPERO How now? Moody?
What is't thou canst demand?

ARIEL My liberty.

PROSPERO Before the time be out? No more!

ARIEL (*Sits*) I prithee,
Remember I have done thee worthy service,
Told thee no lies, made me no mistakings, served
Without or grudge or grumblings. Thou did
promise to bate* me a full year.

PROSPERO Dost thou forget
From what a torment I did free thee?

ARIEL I do not, sir.

PROSPERO (*Rises*) Thou liest, malignant thing! Hast thou forgot
The foul witch Sycorax, who with age and envy*
Was grown into a hoop? Hast thou forgot her?

ARIEL No, sir.

Bermoothes: Bermuda **float**: sea **pains**: duties **remember**: remind **bate**: reduce my term of service **envy**: malice

PROSPERO Thou hast. Where was she born? Speak!
    Tell me!

ARIEL (*Kneels before* PROSPERO) Sir, in Argier.*

PROSPERO O, was she so? I must
    Once in a month recount what thou hast been,
    Which thou forget'st. This damned witch Sycorax,
    For mischiefs manifold and sorceries terrible
    To enter human hearing, from Argier,

PROSPERO Thou know'st, was banished. For one thing she did
    They would not take her life. Is not this true?

ARIEL (*Rises*) Ay, sir.

PROSPERO This blue-eyed* hag was hither brought with child
    And here was left by th' sailors. Thou, my slave,
    As thou report'st thyself, wast then her servant.
    Imprisoned thou didst painfully remain
    A dozen years; within which space she died
    And left thee there, where thou didst vent thy groans
    As fast as millwheels strike. Then was this island-
    (Save for the son that she did litter here,
    A freckled whelp, hag-born) not honored with
    A human shape.

ARIEL Yes, Caliban her son.

PROSPERO Dull thing, I say so.

ARIEL (*Kneels before* PROSPERO) I thank thee, master.

PROSPERO If thou more murmur'st, I will rend an oak
    And peg thee in his* knotty entrails till
    Thou hast howled away twelve winters.

Argier: Algiers   **blue-eyed**: dark circles around her eyes   **his**: its

ARIEL Pardon, master.
(*Rises*) I will be correspondent* to command
And do my spiriting gently.*

PROSPERO Do so; and after two days
I will discharge thee.

ARIEL That's my noble master!
What shall I do? Say what? What shall I do?

PROSPERO Go make thyself like a nymph o' th' sea. Be subject
To no sight but thine and mine, invisible
To every eyeball else.* Go take this shape
And hither come in 't. Go! Hence with diligence!

Exit ARIEL.

PROSPERO Awake, dear heart, awake! Thou hast slept well.
Awake!

MIRANDA The strangeness of your story put
Heaviness in me.

PROSPERO Shake it off. Come on.
(*He helps her up.*) We'll visit Caliban, my slave, who never
Yields us kind answer.

MIRANDA 'Tis a villain, sir,
I do not love to look on.

PROSPERO But as 'tis,
We cannot miss* him. He does make our fire,
Fetch in our wood, and serves in offices
That profit us. What, ho! Slave! Caliban!
Thou earth, thou! Speak!

---

correspondent: obedient   **gently:** gladly perform my duties   **eyeball else:** invisible to everyone but Prospero   **miss:** do without

CALIBAN (*Off stage*) There's wood enough within.

PROSPERO Come forth, I say! There's other business for thee.
　　Come thou tortoise!

Enter ARIEL *dressed as a water nymph.*

PROSPERO Fine apparition! My quaint* Ariel,
　　Hark in thine ear.

ARIEL My lord it shall be done.

ARIEL *crosses to the edge of the stage.*

PROSPERO (*to* CALIBAN) Thou poisonous slave, got by the devil
　　himself upon thy wicked* dam, come forth!

ARIEL *is pulling an invisible cord as* CALIBAN *enters as if drawn in.*

CALIBAN As wicked dew as e'er my mother brushed
　　With raven's feather from unwholesome fen
　　Drop on you both! A southwest blow* on ye
　　And blister you all o'er!

PROSPERO For this, be sure, tonight thou shalt have cramps,
　　Side-stitches that shall pen thy breath up. Urchins*
　　Shall, for that vast of night that they may work,*
　　All exercise on thee.

CALIBAN (*Sits*) I must eat my dinner,
　　Thy island's mine by Sycorax my mother,
　　Which thou tak'st from me. When thou cam'st first,
　　Thou strok'st me and made much of me; wouldst give me
　　Water with berries in 't; and teach me how

---

quaint: clever **wicked:** harmful **southwest blow:** a wind thought to bring
disease **urchins:** goblins in the shape of hedgehogs **may work:** time of night
when evil spirits are free to conjure

To name the bigger light, and how the less,
That bum by day and night. And then I loved thee
And showed thee all the qualities o' th' isle,
And fresh springs, brine pits, barren place and fertile.
Cursed be I that did so! All the charms
Of Sycorax – toads, beetles, bats, light on you!

PROSPERO Thou most lying slave,
Whom stripes* may move, not kindness! I have used thee
(Filth as thou art) with humane care, and lodged thee
In mine own cell till thou didst seek to violate
The honor of my child.

CALIBAN (*Moves like a wild animal*) O ho, O ho! Would't had been
done! Thou didst prevent me; I had peopled else
This isle with Calibans. (*Sits*)

MIRANDA I pitied thee,
Took pains to make thee speak, taught thee each hour
One thing or other. When thou didst not, savage,
Know thine own meaning, but wouldst gabble like
A thing most brutish, I endowed thy purposes
With words that made them known.

CALIBAN You taught me language, and my profit on 't
Is, I know how to curse. The red plague* rid you
For learning me your language!

PROSPERO Hagseed, hence!
Fetch us in fuel. And be quick, thou 'rt best,*
To answer other business. Shrug'st thou malice?
If thou neglect'st or dost unwillingly
What I command, I'll rack thee with old* cramps,

---

stripes: lashes   **red plague:** plague that produced red sores   **thou 'rt best:** you
had better   **old:** old people's

Fill all thy bones with aches, make thee roar
That beasts shall tremble at thy din.

CALIBAN (*Rise*) No, pray thee.
(*Aside*) I must obey. His art is of such pow'r
It would control my dam's* god, Setebos,
And make a vassal of him.

PROSPERO So, slave; hence!

Exit CALIBAN *and* PROSPERO *in different directions followed by*
MIRANDA. *Enter* ARIEL *singing (playing a flute or tambourine.)*

Enter FERDINAND *as if drawn by an unseen power.*

ARIEL (*sings*)   Come unto these yellow sands,
                                And then take hands.
                    Curtsied when you have and kissed
                            The wild waves whist,*
                        Foot it featly* here and there;
                    And, sweet sprites, the burden bear.

FERDINAND Where should this music be?
This music crept by me upon the waters,
Allaying both their fury and my passion*
With its sweet air. Thence I have followed it,
Or it hath drawn me rather; but 'tis gone.
No, it begins again.

ARIEL (*Singing while standing on a platform above* FERDINAND.)
                        Full fathom five thy father lies;
                        Of his bones are coral made;
                    Those are pearls that were his eyes;
                    Nothing of him that doth fade

dam's: mother's   **whist:** hushed   **featly:** gracefully   **passion:** sorrow

But doth suffer a sea change
Into something rich and strange.

PROSPERO *and* MIRANDA *slowly enter.*

FERDINAND The ditty does remember my drowned father.
This is no mortal business, nor no sound
That the earth owes.* I hear it now above me.

PROSPERO The fringèd curtains of thine eye advance*
And say what thou seest yond.

ARIEL *starts weaving a spell above* FERDINAND.

MIRANDA What is 't? A spirit?
Lord, how it looks about! Believe me, sir,
It carries a brave form. But 'tis a spirit.

PROSPERO No, wench; it eats, and sleeps, and hath such senses
As we have, such. This gallant which thou seest
Was in the wrack; and, but he's something stained
With grief (that's beauty's canker), thou mightst call him
A goodly person. He hath lost his fellows
And strays about to find 'em.

MIRANDA I might call him
A thing divine; for nothing natural
I ever saw so noble.

PROSPERO (*Aside to* ARIEL) Spirit, fine spirit. I'll free
thee within two days for this.

FERDINAND Vouchsafe my prayer
May know if you remain* upon this island,
And that you will some good instruction give
How I may bear me* here. My prime request,

owes: owns   **advance:** raise   **remain:** dwell   **bear me:** conduct myself

Which I do last prounounce, is
(o you wonder!) if you be maid or no?

MIRANDA No wonder, sir,
But certainly a maid.

FERDINAND My language? Heavens!
I am the best of them that speak this speech,
Were I but where 'tis spoken.

PROSPERO How? The best?
What wert thou if the King of Naples heard thee?

FERDINAND A single* thing, as I am now, that wonders
To hear thee speak of Naples. He does hear me,
And that he does I weep. Myself am Naples,
Who with mine eyes, never since at ebb, beheld
The king my father wracked.

MIRANDA Alack, for mercy!

FERDINAND Yes, faith, and all his lords, the Duke of Milan
And his brave son* being twain.*

PROSPERO (*Aside to* ARIEL) The Duke of Milan
And his more braver daughter could control* thee,
If now t'were fit to do 't. At the first sight
They have changed eyes.* Delicate Ariel,
I'll set thee free for this.
(*To* FERDINAND *now firm*) A word, good sir.
I fear you have done yourself some wrong.* A word!

MIRANDA Why speaks my father so ungently? This
Is the third man that e'er I saw, the first

---

single: helpless   **brave son:** only time Antonio is mentioned   **twain:** two
control: refute   **changed eyes:** exchanged loving looks   **done yourself some
wrong:** a polite way of calling him a liar

That e'er I sighed for. Pity move my father
To be inclined my way!

FERDINAND   O, if a virgin,
And your affection not gone forth, I'll make you
The Queen of Naples.

PROSPERO   Soft, sir! One word more.
(*Aside*) They are both in either's pow'rs. But this swift
business
I must uneasy make, lest too light winning
Make the prize light.
(*To* FERDINAND) One word more! I charge thee
That thou attend me. Thou dost here usurp
The name thou ow'st* not, and hast put thyself
Upon this island as a spy, to win it
From me, the lord on 't.

FERDINAND   No, as I am a man!

MIRANDA   There's nothing ill can dwell in such a temple.
If the ill spirit have so fair a house,
Good things will strive to dwell with 't.

PROSPERO   (*To* FERDINAND) Follow me.
(*To* MIRANDA) Speak not you for him. He's a traitor.
(*To* FERDINAND) Come! (*He doesn't move.*)
I'll manacle thy neck and feet together;
Sea water shalt thou drink. Thy food shall be
The fresh-brook mussels, withered roots, and husks
Wherein the acorn cradled. Follow!

FERDINAND   No.
I will resist such entertainment till
Mine enemy has more pow'r.

ow'st: ownest

He draws his sword at PROSPERO *but is magically stopped by* ARIEL.

MIRANDA   O dear father,
> Make not too rash a trial for him, for
> He's gentle and not fearful.*

PROSPERO   What, I say,
> My foot* my tutor?* (*To* FERDINAND) Put thy sword up, traitor,
> Who mak'st a show but dar'st not strike, thy conscience
> Is so possessed with guilt! Come, from thy ward,*
> For I can here disarm thee with this stick*
> And make thy weapon drop.

PROSPERO *gestures, causing* FERDINAND *to drop his sword and freeze.*

MIRANDA   (*Grabbing* PROSPERO) Beseech you, father!

PROSPERO   Hence! Hang not on my garments.

MIRANDA   (*Releasing him*) Sir, have pity.
> I'll be his surety.*

PROSPERO   Silence! One word more
> Shall make me chide thee, if not hate thee. What,
> An advocate for an imposter? Hush!
> Thou think'st there is no more such shapes as he,
> Having seen but him and Caliban?

MIRANDA   My affections
> Are then most humble. I have no ambition
> To see a goodlier man.

PROSPERO   (*To* FERDINAND) Come on, obey!
> Thy nerves* are in their infancy again
> And have no vigor in them.

fearful: cowardly   **foot:** subordinate   **tutor:** inferior   **ward:** defensive position
stick: his magical walking staff   **surety:** one who takes responsibility for another
nerves: sinews

FERDINAND So they are.
> My spirits, as in a dream, are all bound up.
> (*Sits*) My father's loss, the weakness which I feel,
> The wrack of all my friends, nor this man's threats
> To whom I am subdued, are but light to me,
> Behold this maid. (*He takes her hand and kneels before her.*)

PROSPERO (*Aside*) It works.
> (*To* FERDINAND) Come on.
> (*To* ARIEL) Thou hast done well, fine Ariel!
> (*To* FERDINAND) Follow me.
> (*To* ARIEL) Hark what thou else shalt do me.

MIRANDA (*To* FERDINAND) Be of comfort.
> My father's of a better nature, sir.
> Than he appears by speech. This is unwonted
> Which now came from him.

PROSPERO (*To* ARIEL) Thou shalt be free
> As mountain winds; but then* exactly do
> All points of my command.

ARIEL To th' syllable.

PROSPERO (*To* FERDINAND) Come, follow.
> (*To* MIRANDA) Speak not for him.

Exit PROSPERO. MIRANDA *looks at* FERDINAND *for a moment then
exits. As she exits,* FERDINAND *rises and slowly follows, ending* ACT I.

then: till then

ACT II, SCENE 1
ANOTHER PART OF THE ISLAND.

Enter ALONSO, SEBASTIAN, ANTONIO, GONZALO, ADRIAN
and FRANCISCO. ADRIAN *and* FRANCISCO *move in background,*
observing while being entertained.

GONZALO Beseech you, sir, be merry. You have cause
    (So have we all) of joy; for our escape
    Is much beyond our loss. Few in millions
    Can speak like us. Then wisely, good sir, weigh
    Our sorrow with* our comfort.

ALONSO Prithee, peace.

SEBASTIAN (*Aside to* ANTONIO) He receives comfort like cold
    porridge.

ANTONIO (*Aside to* SEBASTIAN) The visitor* will not give him o'er
    so.

SEBASTIAN Look, he's winding up the watch of his wit; by
    and by it will strike.

GONZALO Sir –

ANTONIO Temperance was a delicate wench.

SEBASTIAN Ay, and a subtle, as he most learnedly delivered.

ADRIAN The air breathes upon us here most sweetly.

GONZALO Here is everything advantageous to life.

ANTONIO True; save means to live.

SEBASTIAN Of that there's none, or little.

GONZALO How lush and lusty the grass looks! How green!

with: against   **visitor:** minister who visits the sick

ANTONIO The ground indeed is tawny.

SEBASTIAN With an eye* of green in 't.

ANTONIO He misses not much.

SEBASTIAN No; he doth but mistake the truth totally.

GONZALO But the rarity of it is – which is indeed almost
  beyond credit –

SEBASTIAN As many vouched rarities are.

GONZALO That our garments stained with salt water.

SEBASTIAN I think he will carry this island home in his
  pocket and give it his son for an apple.

ANTONIO Why, in good time.

GONZALO (*To ALONSO*) Sir, we were talking that our garments seem
  now as fresh as when we were at Tunis at the marriage of
  your daughter, Claribel, who is now Queen.
  Is not, sir, my doublet as fresh as the first day I wore it?
  I mean, in a sort?*

ANTONIO That "sort" was well fished for.

GONZALO When I wore it at your daughter's marriage.

ALONSO Would I had never
  Married my daughter there! For, coming thence,
  My son is lost; and, in my rate,* she too,
  Who is so far from Italy removed
  I ne'er again shall see her. O thou mine heir
  Of Naples and of Milan, what strange fish
  Hath made his meal on thee?

eye: spot **a sort:** so to speak **rate:** opinion

25

FRANCISCO (*Kneeling*) Sir, he may live.
   I saw him beat the surges under him
   And ride upon their backs. He trod the water,
   Whose enmity he flung aside, and breasted
   The surge most swol'n that met him.
   I not doubt He came alive to land.

ALONSO No, no, he's gone.

SEBASTIAN (*To ALONSO as FRANCISCO backs away*) Sir,
   you may thank yourself for this great loss,
   That would not bless our Europe with your daughter,
   But rather loose her to an African,
   Where she at least is banished from your eye
   Who hath cause to wet the grief on 't.

ALONSO Prithee, peace.

SEBASTIAN You were kneeled to and importuned otherwise
   By all of us, and the fair soul herself
   Weighed, between loathness and obedience, at
   Which end o' th' beam should bow.* We have lost your son,
   I fear, forever. Milan and Naples have
   Moe* windows in them and of this business' making
   Than we bring men to comfort them.
   The fault's your own.

ALONSO So is the dear'st* o' th' loss.

GONZALO My lord Sebastian,
   The truth you speak doth lack some gentleness,
   And time* to speak it in. You rub the sore
   When you should bring the plaster.

---

bow: her unwillingness to marry and her duty to he father **moe:** more **dear'st:** most heartfelt **time:** appropriate occasion

SEBASTIAN Very well.

GONZALO (*To ALONSO*) It is foul weather in us all, good sir,
    When you are cloudy.

SEBASTIAN (*To ANTONIO*) Foul weather?

ANTONIO Very foul.

SEBASTIAN 'Scape being drunk for want of wine.

GONZALO And women too, but innocent and pure;
    No sovereignty.

SEBASTIAN Yet he would be King on 't.

ANTONIO The latter end of his commonwealth forgets
    the beginning.

GONZALO All things in common nature should produce
    Without sweat or endeavor. Treason, felony,
    Sword, pike,* knife, gun, or need of any engine*
    Would I not have; but nature should bring forth
    Of its own kind, all foison,* all abundance,
    To feed my innocent people.

SEBASTIAN No marrying 'mong his subjects?

ANTONIO None, man, all idle – whores and knaves.

GONZALO I would with such perfection govern, sir,
    T' excel the Golden Age.

SEBASTIAN (*Loudly – drawing his sword*) Save his majesty!

ANTONIO (*Loudly – drawing his sword*) Long live Gonzalo!

GONZALO And – do you mark me, sir?

pike: spear   **engine:** weapon   **foison:** abundance

27

ALONSO Prithee, no more. Thou dost talk nothing to me.

GONZALO I do well believe your Highness; and did it to
minister occasion* to these gentlemen, who are of
such sensible* and nimble lungs that they always
use to laugh at nothing.

ANTONIO *and* SEBASTIAN *engage in swordplay.*

ANTONIO 'Twas you we laughed at.

GONZALO Who in this kind of merry fooling am nothing to
You; so you may continue and laugh at nothing still.

ANTONIO What a blow was there given!

SEBASTIAN An* it not fal'n flatlong.*

GONZALO You are gentlemen of brave mettle. You would lift
the moon out of her sphere if she would continue
in it five weeks without changing.

They sheath their swords as ARIEL *(invisible to them) enters, casting a
spell on* GONZALO, ADRIAN *and* FRANCISCO.

SEBASTIAN We would so, and then go a-batfowling.*

ANTONIO Nay, good my lord, be not angry.

GONZALO No, I warrant you; I will not adventure my
discretion so weakly.* Will you laugh me asleep?
For I am very heavy.

ANTONIO Go sleep, and hear us.

All are asleep except ALONSO, SEBASTIAN *and* ANTONIO.

---

minister occasion: afford opportunity **sensible:** sensitive **an:** if **flat-long:**
with the flat of the sword **a-batfowling:** bird hunting with sticks at night **weakly:**
you, so weak of wit

ALONSO What, all so soon asleep? I wish mine eyes
 Would, with themselves, shut up my thoughts. I find
 They are inclined to do so.

ARIEL starts casting a spell on ALONSO.

SEBASTIAN Please, you, sir,
 Do not omit* the heavy offer of it.
 It seldom visits sorrow; when it doth,
 It is a comforter.

ANTONIO We two, my lord,
 Will guard your person while you take your rest,
 And watch your safety.

ALONSO Thank you. Wondrous heavy.

ALONSO falls gently asleep as ARIEL exits.

SEBASTIAN What a strange drowsiness possesses them!

ANTONIO It is a quality o' th' climate.

SEBASTIAN Why
 Doth it not then our eyelids sink? I find not
 Myself disposed to sleep.

ANTONIO Nor I: my spirits are nimble.
 They fell together all, as by consent.
 My strong imagination sees a crown
 Dropping upon they head.

SEBASTIAN What? Art thou waking?

ANTONIO Do you not hear me speak?

SEBASTIAN I do; and surely
 This is a strange repose, to be asleep

omit: neglect

29

With eyes wide open; standing, speaking, moving,
And yet so fast asleep.

ANTONIO Noble Sebastian,
Thou let'st thy fortune sleep – die, rather; wink'st*
Whiles thou art waking.

SEBASTIAN Thou dost snore distinctly;
Well, I am standing water.

ANTONIO I'll teach you how to flow.

SEBASTIAN Do so. To ebb.
Hereditary sloth instructs me.

ANTONIO Ebbing men indeed
Most often do so near the bottom run
By their own fear or sloth. Thus, sir:
the King his son's alive,
'Tis as impossible that he's undrowned
As he that sleeps here swims.

SEBASTIAN I have no hope
That he's undrowned.

ANTONIO O, out of that no hope
What great hope have you! Will you grant with me
That Ferdinand is drowned?

SEBASTIAN He's gone.

ANTONIO Then tell me,
Who's the next heir of Naples?

SEBASTIAN Claribel.

ANTONIO She that is Queen of Tunis;

wink'st: to shut your eyes

And by that destiny, to perform an act
Whereof what's past is prologue, what to come,
In yours and my discharge.

SEBASTIAN What stuff is this? How say you?
’Tis true my brother's daughter's Queen of Tunis;
So is she heir of Naples; ’twixt which regions
There is some space.

ANTONIO A space whose ev'ry cubit
Seems to cry out "How shall that Claribel
Measure us back to Naples? Keep in Tunis,
And let Sebastian wake!" (*They cross to a private area.*)
Say this were death that now hath seized them,
why, they were no worse than now they are.
As this Gonzalo; I myself could make
A chough* of as deep chat. Oh, that you bore
The mind that I do! What a sleep were this
For your advancement! Do you understand me?

SEBASTIAN Methinks I do.

ANTONIO And how does your content
Tender* your own good fortune?

SEBASTIAN I remember
You did supplant your brother Prospero.

ANTONIO True. And look how well my garments sit upon me,
Much feater* than before. My brother's servants
Were then my fellows; now they are my men.

SEBASTIAN But, for your conscience –

ANTONIO Twenty consciences

chough: a bird that can speak a few words   **tender:** regard   **feater:** more
becomingly

That stand 'twixt me and Milan. Here lies your brother,
No better than the earth he lies upon.

ANTONIO If he were that which now he's like, that's dead* –
(*Draws his dagger*) Whom I, with this obedient steel,
(three inches of it)
Can lay to bed for ever; whiles you, doing thus,
To the perpetual wink* for aye might put
This ancient morsel, this Sir Prudence, who
Should not upbraid our course.

SEBASTIAN Thy case, dear friend,
Shall be my precedent. As thou got'st Milan,
I'll come by Naples. Draw thy sword. One stroke
Shall free thee from the tribute which thou
payest, And I the King shall love thee.

ANTONIO Draw together;
And when I rear my hand, do you the like,
To fall it on Gonzalo.

They draw as ANTONIO *sheaths his dagger.*

SEBASTIAN O, but one word!

They freeze.

Enter ARIEL *(invisible)*

ARIEL My master through his art foresees the danger
That you, his friend, are in, and sends me forth
(for else his project dies) to keep them living.

ARIEL *sings in* GONZALO's *ear:*
Whilst you were here do snoring lie,
Open-eyed conspiracy

that's dead: that is, if he were dead   **wink:** sleep

His time doth take.
If of life you keep a care,
Shake off slumber and beware.
(*Hums in his ear.*)
Awake, awake!

(*SEBASTIAN and ANTONIO are now free to move.*)

ANTONIO Then let us both be sudden.

GONZALO (*Waking*) Now good angels Preserve the king!

(*The others wake.*)

ALONSO Why, how now? Ho, awake!
Why are you drawn?
Wherefore this ghastly looking?

GONZALO What's the matter?

SEBASTIAN *is trying to come up with a response.*

SEBASTIAN Whiles we stood here securing your repose,
Even now, we heard a hollow burst of bellowing
Like bulls, or rather lions. Did't not wake you?
It struck mine ear most terribly.

ALONSO I heard nothing.
Heard you this, Gonzalo?

GONZALO Upon mine honor, sir, I heard a humming,
And that a strange one too, which did awake me.

ALONSO (*Rising*) Lead off this ground, and let's make further search
For my poor son. (*He draws his sword.*)

GONZALO (*ALL OTHERS rise*) Heavens keep him from these beasts!
For he is, sure, i' th' island.

ALONSO Lead away.

ARIEL remains as ALL OTHERS exit following SEBASTIAN.

ARIEL   Prospero my lord shall know what I have done.
   So, King, go safely on to seek thy son.

Exit ARIEL.

ACT II, SCENE 2
ANOTHER PART OF THE ISLAND.

Pounding thunder as CALIBAN *enters with an armful of woodcuttings.*

CALIBAN All the infections that the sun sucks up
From bogs, fens, flats, on Prosper fall, and make him
By inchmeal* a disease!

Enter TRINCULO.

Lo, now, lo!
Here comes a spirit of his, and to torment me
For bringing wood in slowly. I'll fall flat.
Perchance he will not mind me.

CALIBAN *lies down beneath his exceedingly long cloak.*

TRINCULO Here's neither bush nor shrub to bear off* any weather at
all. What have we here? A man or a fish? Dead
Or alive? A fish! He smells like a fish.
(*Uncovers* CALIBAN'*s feet*) Legged like a man!
(*Uncovers a arm*) And his fins like arms! This
is no fish, but an islander that hath lately suffered by thunder-
bolt. (*Thunder*) Misery acquaints a man with
strange bedfellows. I will here shroud till the
dregs of the storm be past.

Lies beneath CALIBAN'*s cloak so they become one very long person.*

Enter STEPHANO *drunk and singing with bottle in hand.*

STEPHANO I shall no more to sea, to sea;
Here shall I die ashore.
This is a very scurvy tune to sing at a man's funeral.
Well, here's my comfort. (*Drinks*)

---

inchmeal: inch by inch   **bear off:** ward off

he master, the swabber, the boatswain, and I,
The gunner and his mate,
Loved Mall, Meg, and Marian, and Margery
But none of us cared for Kate.
For she had a tongue with a tang,
Would cry to a sailor "Go hang!"
She loved not the savor of tar nor of pitch;
Yet a tailor might scratch her where'er she did itch.
Then to sea, boys, and let her go hang!
This is a scurvy tune too; but here's my comfort. (*Drinks*)

CALIBAN   Do not torment me! O!

His arms jut out in front of him with TRINCULO's *feet from the other end.*

STEPHANO   (*Startled*) What's the matter? Have we devils here?
I have not scaped drowning to be afeard now
of your four legs. If I can recover* him,
and keep him tame, and get to Naples with him,
he's a present for any emperor that ever trod
on neat's* leather.

CALIBAN   (*Their hands and feet are shaking.*) Do not torment me,
prithee. I'll bring my wood home faster.

STEPHANO   He in his fit now and does not talk after
the wisest. He shall taste of my bottle; if he have
never drunk wine afore, it will go near to remove
his fit. He shall pay for him that hath him, and that soundly.

CALIBAN   Thou dost me yet but little hurt.

STEPHANO   Come on your ways, open your mouth;
here is that which will give language to you, cat.*

---

recover: cure   **neat's:** cow   **cat:** proverb: "Good liquor will make a cat speak."

Open your mouth. This will shake your shaking.
(*Gives* CALIBAN *drink*) You cannot tell who's your friend.
Open your chaps* again.

TRINCULO (*Sticking his head out*) I should know that voice.
It should be – but he is drowned, and these are devils.
O, defend me!

STEPHANO Four legs and two voices – a most delicate
monster! His forward voice now is to speak well of
his friend; his backward voice is to utter foul
speeches and to detract. Come! (*Gives him drink*)
Amen! I will pour some in thy other mouth.

TRINCULO Stephano!

STEPHANO (*Steps back*) Doth thy other mouth call me? Mercy,
mercy! This is a devil, and no monster. I will leave
him; I have no long spoon.* (*He starts to leave.*)

TRINCULO Stephano! If thou beest Stephano, touch me and
speak to me; for I am Trinculo – be not afeared.

STEPHANO If thou beest Trinculo, come forth. I'll pull
thee by the lesser legs. If any be Trinculo's legs,
these are they. (*Draws him from the cloak.*)
Thou art very Trinculo indeed!
How cam'st thou to be the siege* of this mooncalf?*

TRINCULO I took him to be killed with a thunderstroke. But art
thou not drowned, Stephano? I hope now thou art
not drowned. I hid me under the dead mooncalf's
gabberdine for fear of the storm. And art thou living,
Stephano? O Stephano, two Neapolitans scaped!

---

chaps: jaws   **spoon:** proverb: "He who sups with the devil must have a long
spoon."   **siege:** excrement   **mooncalf:** monstrosity long

Whirls STEPHANO around out of joy.

STEPHANO Prithee do not turn me about; my stomach is not constant. (*TRINCULO seats him and sits next to him.*)

CALIBAN (*Aside*) These be fine things, and if* they be not sprites. That's a brave god and bears celestial liquor. I will kneel to him. (*He does.*)

STEPHANO How didst thou scape? How cam'st thou hither? I escaped upon a butt of sack which the sailors heaved o'erboard – by this bottle which I made of the bark of a tree with mine own hands since I was cast ashore.

CALIBAN (*Rises*) I'll swear upon that bottle to be thy true subject, for the liquor is not earthly.

STEPHANO Here. Swear then how thou escap'dst.

TRINCULO (*Rises*) Swum ashore, man, like a duck. I can swim like a duck, I'll be sworn.

STEPHANO Here, kiss the book. (*Gives him a drink*) Though thou canst swim like a duck, thou art made like a goose.

TRINCULO O Stephano, hast any more of this?

STEPHANO The whole butt, man. My cellar is in a rock by th' seaside, where my wine is hid.

CALIBAN Hast thou not dropped from heaven?

STEPHANO Out o' th' moon, I do assure thee. I was the man i' th' moon when time was.*

CALIBAN I have seen thee in her, and I do adore thee.

and if: if   **when time was:** once upon a time

38

My mistress showed me thee, and thy dog, and
thy bush.*

STEPHANO Come, swear to that; kiss the book. (*Gives him drink*)

TRINCULO (*Aside*) By this good light, this is a very shallow monster! I
afeard of him? A very weak monster!

CALIBAN I'll show thee every fertile inch o' th' island;
and I will kiss thy foot. I prithee, be my god.

TRINCULO (*Aside*) By this light, a most perfidious and drunken
Monster! When god's asleep, he'll rob his bottle.

CALIBAN I'll kiss thy foot. I'll swear myself thy subject.

STEPHANO Come on then. Down, and swear!

TRINCULO (*Aside*) I shall laugh myself to death at this puppy-headed
monster. A most scurvy monster!

STEPHANO Come, kiss. (CALIBAN *drinks.*)

TRINCULO But that the poor monster's in drink. An
abominable monster!

CALIBAN I'll show thee the best springs; I'll pluck thee berries;
A plague upon the tyrant that I serve!
I'll bear him no more sticks, but follow thee.
Thou wondrous man.

TRINCULO (*Aside*) A most ridiculous monster, to make a wonder of a
poor drunkard!

CALIBAN I Prithee let me bring thee where crabs* grow;
And I with my long nails will dig the pignuts,*

and thy bush: the Man in the Moon was banished for gathering brush with this
dog **crabs**: crab apples **pignuts**: peanuts

Show thee a jay's nest, and instruct thee how
to snare the nimble marmoset. Wilt thou go with me?

STEPHANO I prithee now, lead the way without any more
talking. Trinculo, the Kind and all our company
else bring drowned, we will inherit here.
Here, bear my bottle. (*He hands* CALIBAN *a drink*)
(*Aside*) Fellow Trinculo, we'll fill him by and by again.

CALIBAN (*Sings drunkenly*) No more dams I'll make for fish,
nor fetch in firing at requiring,
Nor scrape trenchering,* nor wash dish.
'Ban, 'Ban, Ca – Caliban
Has a new master. Get a new man.
Freedom, high day! High day, freedom! Freedom
high day, freedom!

STEPHANO O brave monster! Lead the way.

ALL *exit drunk and laughing, bringing* ACT II *to a conclusion.*

trenchering: wooden plates

ACT III, SCENE 1
IN FRONT OF PROSPERO'S CELL.

Enter FERDINAND *bearing two logs and places them down.*

FERDINAND The mistress which I serve quickens* what's dead
    and makes my labors pleasures. (*Sits*) O, she is
    Ten times more gentle than her father's crabbed,
    And he's composed of harshness. I must remove
    Some thousands of these logs and pile them up,
    Upon a sore injunction.*
    (*Lift his logs and rises.*)

Enter MIRANDA *with* PROSPERO. PROSPERO *is unseen and holds a
large book.*

MIRANDA Alas, now pray you, work not so hard!
    Pray set it down and rest you. When this bums,
    'Twill weep* for having wearied you. My father
    Is hard at study; pray now rest yourself.

FERDINAND O most dear mistress,
    The sun will set before I shall discharge
    What I must strive to do.

MIRANDA If you'll sit down
    I'll bear your logs the while. Pray give me that;
    I'll carry it to the pile.

FERDINAND No, precious creature,
    I had rather crack my sinews, break my back,
    Than you should such dishonor undergo
    While I sit lazy by.

MIRANDA It would become me
    As well as it does you; and I should do it

quickens: brings to life **sore injunction:** severe command **weep:** exude resin

With much more ease, for my good will is to it,
And yours it is against.

PROSPERO (*Aside*) Poor worm, thou art infected!
This visitation* shows it.

MIRANDA You look wearily.

FERDINAND No, noble mistress, 'tis fresh morning with me
When you are by at night.* I do beseech you,
Chiefly that I might set it in my prayers,
What is your name?

MIRANDA Miranda. O my father,
I have broke your hest* to say so!

FERDINAND Admired* Miranda!
Indeed the top of admiration, worth
What's dearest to the world!
So perfect and so peerless, are created
Of every creature's best.

MIRANDA I do not know
One of my sex; no woman's face remember. Nor have I seen
More that I may call men than you, good friend,
And my dear father. I would not wish
Any companion in the world but you;
But I prattle something too wildly,
and my father's precepts I therein do forget.

FERDINAND I am, in my condition
A prince, Miranda; I do think, a king
(I would not so), and would do no more endure
This wooden slavery than to suffer

---

visitation: infection **at night:** when you are tired **hest:** command **admired:** wonderful

The fleshfly blow my mouth. (*Takes her hand*)
Hear my soul speak!
The very instant that I saw you, did
My heart fly to your service.

MIRANDA Do you love me?

FERDINAND O heaven, O earth, bear witness to this sound,
Beyond all limit of what else i' th' world,
(*On bended knee*) Do love, prize, honor you.

PROSPERO (*Aside*) Fair encounter
Of two most rare affections! Heavens rain grace
On that which breeds between 'em!

MIRANDA I am your wife, if you will marry me;
If not, I'll die your maid. To be your fellow*
You may deny me; but I'll be your servant,
Whether you will or no.

FERDINAND (*Rises*) My mistress, dearest, and I thus humble ever.

MIRANDA My husband then?

FERDINAND Ay, with a heart as willing
As bondage e'er of freedom.* Here's my hand.

MIRANDA And mine, with my heart in 't. And now farewell
Till half an hour hence.

FERDINAND A thousand thousand!*

FERDINAND *and* MIRANDA *exit in different directions.*

PROSPERO So glad of this as they I cannot be,
Who are surprised withal.* But my rejoicing

---

fellow: equal   **e'er of freedom:** over freedom   **thousand thousand:** a million
goodbyes   **withal:** by it

At nothing can be more. I'll to my book;
For yet ere suppertime must I perform
Much business appertaining.*

appertaining: for my plans

ACT III, SCENE 2
Another Part Of The Island.

Enter CALIBAN, STEPHANO *and* TRINCULO *all drunk.*

STEPHANO Tell not me. When the butt is out, we will drink
water; not a drop before. Therefore bear up and
board'em!* Servant monster, drink to me.

TRINCULO Servant monster? The folly of this island! They
say there's but five upon this isle; we are three of
them. If th' other two be brained like us, the state
totters.

STEPHANO Drink, servant monster, when I bid thee; thy eyes
are almost set in thy head.

TRINCULO *(Sits)* Where should they be set else? He were a brave
monster indeed if they were set in his tail.

STEPHANO *(Sits)* My man-monster hath drowned his tongue in
sack. Thou shalt be my lieutenant, monster, or my standard.*

TRINCULO Your lieutenant, if you list;* he's no standard.

CALIBAN How does thy honor? Let me lick thy shoe.
    (indicating TRINCULO*)* I'll not serve him; he is not valiant.

STEPHANO *lifts his foot and* CALIBAN *kisses it.*

TRINCULO Thou liest, most ignorant monster; I am in
case* to justle* a constable. Why, thou
deboshed* fish thou, was there ever man a
coward that hath drunk so much sack as I today?

CALIBAN *(Rise)* Lo, how he mocks me! Wilt thou let him, my lord?

---

board'em: stand firm and attack   **standard:** standard bearer   **list:** a pun for
leaning over one side of the ship **case:** fit condition **justle:** jostle **deboshed:**
debauched

46

TRINCULO "Lord" quoth he? That a monster should be such a
    natural!*

CALIBAN Lo, lo, again! Bite him to death, I prithee.

STEPHANO (*Sits*) Trinculo, keep a good tongue in your head. If you
    prove a mutineer – the next tree!* The poor
    monster's my subject, and he shall not suffer
    indignity.

CALIBAN I thank my noble lord. Wilt thou be pleased to
    hearken once again to the suit I made to thee?

STEPHANO Marry,* will I. Kneel and repeat it; I will stand,
    and so shall Trinculo.

ARIEL enters unseen as STEPHANO *rises and urges* TRINCULO *to rise.*

CALIBAN As I told thee before, I am subject to a
    tyrant, A sorcerer, that by his cunning hath
    Cheated me of the island.

ARIEL Thou liest.

CALIBAN Thou liest, thou jesting monkey thou!
    I would my valiant master would destroy thee.
    I do not lie.

TRINCULO Why I said nothing.

STEPHANO Mum then, and no more. Proceed.

CALIBAN I say by sorcery he got this isle;
    From me he got it.

STEPHANO That's most certain.

CALIBAN Thou shalt be lord of it, and I'll serve thee.

natural: idiot **the next tree:** you will hang **marry:** indeed

STEPHANO How now shall this be compassed?
>   Canst thou bring me to the party?

CALIBAN Yea, yea, my lord! I'll yield him thee asleep,
>   Where thou mayst knock a nail into his head.

ARIEL Thou liest; thou canst not.

CALIBAN What a pied* ninny's this! Thou scurvy patch!*
>   I do beseech thy greatness, give him blows.

STEPHANO Trinculo, run into no further danger!

TRINCULO Why, what did I? I did nothing. I'll go farther off.

STEPHANO Didst thou not say he lied?

ARIEL Thou liest.

STEPHANO Do I so? Take thou that! (*Strikes* TRINCULO)
>   As you like this, give me the lie another time.

TRINCULO I did not give the lie. Out o' your wits, and hearing
>   too? A pox o' your bottle!

CALIBAN Ha, ha, ha!

STEPHANO Now forward with your tale. (*To* TRINCULO)
>   Prithee, stand further off.

CALIBAN Beat him enough. After a little time,
>   I'll beat him too.

STEPHANO Stand farther. (*To* CALIBAN) Come, proceed.

CALIBAN Why, as I told thee, 'tis a custom with him
>   I' th afternoon to sleep. There thou mayst brain him,
>   Batter his skull, or paunch* him with a stake,
>   Remember first to possess his books; for without them,

pied: foolish   **scurvy patch:** fool   **paunch:** stab in the stomach

48

He's but a sot,* as I am, nor hath not
One spirit to command.

STEPHANO Is it so brave a lass?

CALIBAN Ay, lord. She will become thy bed, I warrant,
And bring thee forth brave brood.

STEPHANO Monster, I will kill this man. His daughter and I will
be King and Queen – and Trinculo
and thyself shall be viceroys.

TRINCULO Excellent.

STEPHANO Give me thy hand. I am sorry I beat thee; but while
thou liv'st, keep a good tongue in thy head.

CALIBAN Within this half hour will he be asleep. Wilt thou
destroy him then?

STEPHANO Ay, on mine honor.

ARIEL This will I tell my master.

CALIBAN Thou mak'st me merry; I am full of pleasure.
Let us be jocund. Will you troll the catch*
You taught me but whilere?*

STEPHANO At thy request, monster, I will do reason, Any reason.*
Come on, Trinculo, let us sing. (*Sings*)
Flout *'em and scout* *'em*
And scout 'em and flout 'em!
Thought is free.

CALIBAN That's not the tune.

ARIEL *plays a tune.*

sot: fool **Troll the catch:** sing the round **but whilere:** a short time ago **any reason:** anything within reason **flout:** deride **scout:** jeer at

STEPHANO If thou beest a man, show thyself in thy likeness.
If thou beest a devil, tak'st as thou list.

CALIBAN Art thou afeard?

STEPHANO No, monster, not I.

CALIBAN Be not afeard; the isle is full of noises.
Sounds and sweet airs that give delight and hurt not.
The clouds methought would open and show riches
Ready to drop upon me, that, when I waked
I cried to dream again.

STEPHANO This will prove a brave kingdom to me, where I
shall have my music for nothing.

CALIBAN When Prospero is destroyed.

STEPHANO That shall be by and by; I remember the story.

Exit ARIEL with music fading.

TRINCULO The sound is going away. Let's follow it, and after
do our work.

STEPHANO Lead monster; we'll follow. I would I could see this
Taborer; he lays it on.

TRINCULO (*To CALIBAN*) Wilt come? I'll follow, Stephano.

Exit STEPHANO, TRINCULO and CALIBAN.

ACT III, SCENE 3
ANOTHER PART OF THE ISLAND

Enter ALONSO, SEBASTIAN, ANTONIO, GONZALO, ADRIAN and
FRANCISCO.

GONZALO By'r lakin,* I can go no further, sir;
    I needs must rest me.

ALONSO Old lord, I cannot blame thee,
    Who am myself attached* with wearinesss
    Top th' dulling of my spirits. Sit down and rest.

GONZALO sits. ANTONIO and SEBASTIAN sit next to each other as
FRANCISCO and SEBASTIAN remain near one another.

ALONSO Even here I will put off my hope, and keep it
    No longer for my flatterer. He is drowned
    Whom thus we stray to find; and the sea mocks
    Our frustrate search on land. Well, let him go.

ANTONIO (*Aside to SEBASTIAN*) I am right glad that he's so out of
    hope.
    Do not for one repulse forgo the purpose
    That you resolved t' effect.

SEBASTIAN (*Aside to ANTONIO*) The next advantage
    Will we take thoroughly.

ANTONIO (*Aside to SEBASTIAN*) Let it be tonight;
    For now they are oppressed with travel, they
    Will not nor cannot use such vigilance
    As when they are fresh.

SEBASTIAN (*Aside to ANTONIO*) I say tonight. No more.

PROSPERO enters and remains unseen upstage while, along with strange

by'r lakin: by our lady   **attached:** seized

music, a banquet table is brought on by sprites that beckon ALONSO *to eat.* ALL *rise and gather and after the sprite dance they depart.*

ALONSO What harmony is this? My good friends, hark!

SEBASTIAN A living drollery.* Now I will believe
    That there are unicorns; that in Arabia
    There is one tree, the phoenix' throne; one phoenix
    At this hour reigning there.

ANTONIO I'll believe both;
    And what does else want credit,* come to me,
    And I'll be sworn 'tis true. Travelers ne'er did lie,
    Though fools at home condemn 'em.

GONZALO If in Naples
    I should report this now, would they believe me?

PROSPERO (*Aside*) Honest lord,
    Thou hast said well; for some of you there present
    Are worse than devils.

ALONSO I cannot too much muse*
    Such shapes, such gesture, and such sound, expressing
    (Although they want the use of tongue) a kind
    Of excellent dumb discourse.

PROSPERO (*Aside*) Praise in departing.*

ALL *gather around the table.*

FRANCISCO They vanished strangely.

SEBASTIAN No matter, since
    They have left their viands* behind; for we have stomachs.
    Will't please you taste of what is here?

drollery: puppet show **credit:** believing **muse:** wonder **praise in departing:** save your praise for the end **viands:** foodstuff

ALONSO Not I.

GONZALO Faith, sir, you need not fear. When we were boys,
    Who would believe there were such men
    Whose heads stood in their breasts?

ALONSO I will stand to and feed;
    Although my last, no matter, since I feel
    The best is past. Brother, my lord the Duke,
    Stand to, and do as we.

Thunder and lightning as ARIEL *enters (for now seen by all) dressed
with large wings, stands upon the table speaking in a menacing tone.*

ARIEL You are three men of sin, being most unfit to live.
    I have made you mad.

They draw their swords.

ARIEL You fools! I and my fellows are ministers of Fate.
    My fellow ministers are like invulnerable. If you could hurt,*
    Your swords are now too massy* for your strengths.
    But remember that you three from Milan did supplant good
    Prospero; Exposed unto the sea, which hath requit it.*
    Him and his innocent child. For which foul deed
    The pow'rs, delaying, not forgetting, have
    Incensed the seas and shores, yea, all the creatures,
    Against your peace. Thee of thy son, Alonso,
    They have bereft; and do pronounce by me ling'ring
    perdition.*
    Upon your heads, is nothing but heart's sorrow*
    And a clear life ensuing.

*ARIEL *vanishes in thunder as the table is removed.* ALL *sheath their
swords.*

If you could hurt: even if you could hurt us   **massy:** heavy   **requit it:** avenged
that crime   **perdition:** punishment   **heart's sorrow:** only repenting

GONZALO I' th' name of something holy, sir, why stand you
  In this strange stare?

ALONSO O, it is monstrous, monstrous!
  Methought the billows spoke and told me of it;
  The thunder, that deep and dreadful organ pipe, pronounced
  The name of Prosper; It did bass my trespass.*
  Therefore my son i' th' ooze is bedded; and
  I'll seek him deeper than e'er plummet sounded
  And with him there lie mudded. (ALONSO *exits.*)

SEBASTIAN But one fiend at a time,
  I'll fight their legions o'er!

ANTONIO I'll be thy second.

Exit SEBASTIAN *and* ANTONIO.

GONZALO All three of them are desperate; their great guilt,
  Like poison given to work a great time after,
  Follow them swiftly
  And hinder them from what this ecstasy*
  May now provoke them to.

ADRIAN Follow, I pray you.

Exit ALL *but* PROSPERO.

PROSPERO Bravely the figure of this harpy hast thou
  Performed, my Ariel; a grace it had, devouring.*
  Of my instruction hast thou nothing bated*
  So with good life*
  And observation strange, my meaner ministers*

---

bass my trespass: helped me understand **ecstasy**: madness **devouring**: making
the banquet disappear **bated**: omitted **good life**: realistic acting **meaner
minister**: inferior to Ariel

Their several kinds have done.* They now are in my pow'r.
Young Ferdinand, whom they suppose is drowned,
And his and mine loved darling.

Exit PROSPERO, *ending* ACT III.

done: well acted their parts

ACT IV, SCENE 1
IN FRONT OF PROSPERO'S CELL.

Enter PROSPERO, MIRANDA and FERDINAND.

PROSPERO (*Arm around MIRANDA*)
If I have too austerely punished you,
Your compensation makes amends; for I
Have given you here a third of mine own life, all thy
Vexations were but my trial of thy love, and thou
Hast strangely* stood the test. Here, afore heaven,
I ratify this my rich gift. (*Prod MIRANDA towards FERDINAND*)
Take my daughter. But (*x between FERDINAND and MIRANDA*)
If thou dost break her virgin-knot before
All sanctimonious* ceremonies may
With full and holy rite be minist'red,
No sweet aspersion* shall the heavens let fall
To make this contract grow.*

FERDINAND As I hope
For quiet days, fair issue, and long life,
With such love as 'tis now, shall never melt
Mine honor into lust.

PROSPERO Fairly spoke
Sit then and talk with her; she is thine own.
What, Ariel!* My industrious servant, Ariel!

Enter ARIEL.

ARIEL What would my potent master? Here I am.

PROSPERO Go bring the rabble,* for I must
Bestow upon the eyes of this young couple

---

strangely: wonderfully **sanctimonious:** holy **aspersion:** blessing **grow:**
become fruitful **what Ariel:** summoning Ariel **rabble:** shabbier fellows

Some vanity of mine art. It is my promise,
And they expect it from me.

ARIEL Presently?

PROSPERO Ay, with a twink.*

ARIEL Before you can say "Come" and "Go,"
Will be here with mop and mow.*
Do you love me, master? No?

PROSPERO Dearly my delicate Ariel. Do not approach
Till thou dost hear me call.

ARIEL (*Sadly*) Well; I conceive.* (ARIEL *exits.*)

PROSPERO Look thou be true. Do not give dalliance
Too much the rein; the strongest oaths are straw
To th' fire i' th' blood. Be more abstemious,*
Or else, goodnight your vow!

FERDINAND I warrant you, sir.
The white cold virgin snow upon my heart
Abates the ardor of my liver.*

PROSPERO Well, now come, my Ariel; Bring a corollary.*
Rather than want a spirit. Appear, and pertly!
No tongue! All eyes! Be silent. (*Soft music*)

Exit ARIEL *immediately after leading* IRIS *onto the stage.* IRIS *is
wearing and carrying flowers. (Singing her lines is optional.)*

IRIS Ceres, most bounteous lady, thy rich leas*
Of wheat, rye, barley, oats and peas;
Thy turfy mountains, where live nibbling sheep,

---

twink: twinkling of the eye **mop and mow:** gestures and grimaces **conceive:**
understand **abstemious:** moderate **my liver:** sexual passions **a corollary:**
an extra **rich leas:** meadows

And flat meads thatched with stover,* them to keep;
Thy sea-marge, sterile and rocky-hard,
Where thou thyself dost air – the Queen o' th' sky.*
Bids thee leave these, and with her sovereign grace,
ere on this grass plot, in this very place,
To come and sport; her peacocks fly amain.*
Approach, rich Ceres, her to entertain.

move a bunch and be dramatic

Enter CERES *singing her lines and wearing flowers.*

CERES Hail, many-colored messenger. Why hath thy queen
Summoned me hither to this short-grassed green?

IRIS A contract of true love to celebrate
And some donation freely to estate*
On the blessed lovers.

CERES Tell me, heavenly bow,
If Venus or her son, as thou dost know,
Do now attend the Queen?

IRIS Of her society be not afraid.

CERES Highest queen of state,
Great Juno, comes; I know her by her gait.

Enter JUNO *singing her lines while wearing flowers.*

JUNO   Honor, riches, marriage blessing,
                   Long continuance, and increasing,
                      Hourly joys be still* upon you!
                   Juno sings her blessings on you.

circle & dance around couple

FERDINAND This is a most majestic vision, and
Harmonious charmingly. May I be bold
To think these spirits?

---

stover: kind of grass **th' sky:** Juno **amain:** swiftly **estate:** bestow **still:** forever

PROSPERO Spirits, which by mine art
    I have from their confines called to enact
    My present fancies.

FERDINAND Let me live here ever!
    So rare a wond'red* father and a wise
    Makes this place Paradise.

CERES whispers IRIS should give flowers to MIRANDA. IRIS does so.

*CERES, JUNO and IRIS dance around MIRANDA and FERDINAND.
Other sprites might enter and join them in the dance. After awhile all
freeze.*

PROSPERO I had forgot that foul conspiracy
    Of the beast Caliban and his confederates
    Against my life. The minute of their plot
    Is almost come. (*To the SPIRITS*) Well done! (keep dancing)
    (*Angrily*) Avoid!* No more!

(*CERES, IRIS, JUNO disappear.*)

FERDINAND This is strange. Your father's in some passion
    That works him strongly.

MIRANDA Never till this day
    Saw I him touched with anger so distempered.*

PROSPERO Be cheerful, sir.
    Our revels now are ended. These our actors,
    As I foretold you, were all spirits and
    Are melted into air, into thin air; We are such stuff
    As dreams are made on, and our little life
    Is rounded with a sleep. (*X to FERDINAND*) Sir, I am vexed.

wond'red: wonderful **avoid:** be gone **distempered:** violent

PROSPERO (*Reaches to* MIRANDA) If you be pleased, retire into my
  cell
  And there repose. A turn or two I'll walk
  To still my beating mind. (*Indicating they should leave.*)

MIRANDA We wish you peace.

(FERDINAND *follows* MIRANDA *out.*)

Enter ARIEL.

ARIEL What's thy pleasure?

PROSPERO Spirit, we must prepare to meet with Caliban.

ARIEL Ay, my commander. When I presented* Ceres,
  I thought to have told thee of it, but I feared
  Lest I might anger thee.

PROSPERO Say again, where didst thou leave these varlets?*

ARIEL I told you, sir, they were red-hot with drinking;
  So full of valor that they smote the air. At last I left them
  I' th' filthy mantled* pool beyond your cell.

PROSPERO This was well done, my bird.
  Thy shape invisible retain thou still.
  The trumpery* in my house, go bring it hither
  For stale to catch these thieves.

ARIEL I go, I go.

Exit ARIEL.

PROSPERO A born devil on whose nature
  Nurture can never stick; on whom my pains,
  Humanely taken, all, all lost, quite lost!

presented: acted the part of   **varlets:** ruffians   **mantled:** covered with filth
trumpery: glistening apparel

And as is with age his body uglier grows,
So his mind cankers. I will plague them all,
Even to roaring.

ARIEL *immediately enters hanging cloaks, hats and glistening apparel.*

PROSPERO Come, hang them on this line.

PROSPERO *and* ARIEL *remain invisible as* CALIBAN, STEPHANO *and*
TRINCULO *enter drunk.*

CALIBAN Pray you tread softly, that the blind mole may not
Hear a foot fall. We now are near his cell.

STEPHANO (*Sits*) Monster, your fairy, which you say is a harmless
fairy, has done little better than played the Jack* with us.

TRINCULO Monster, I do smell all horse piss, at which my
nose is in great indignation. (*Sits*)

STEPHANO So is mine. Do you hear, monster? If I
Should take a displeasure against you, look you –

TRINCULO Thou wert but a lost monster.

CALIBAN Be patient for the prize I'll bring thee to
Shall hoodwink* this mischance. Therefore,
speak softly.

STEPHANO There is not only disgrace and dishonor in that,
monster, but an infinite loss. I will fetch my bottle. (*He rises.*)

CALIBAN Prithee, my king, be quiet. Seest thou here?
This is the mouth o' th' cell. No noise, and enter.

STEPHANO Give me thy hand. I do begin to have bloody thoughts.

jack: practical joker   **hoodwink:** put out of sight

TRINCULO (*x's to clothes*) O king Stephano! Look what a wardrobe
here is for thee!

CALIBAN Let it alone, thou fool! It is but trash.

STEPHANO Put off that gown, Trinculo! By this hand,
I'll have that gown!

TRINCULO Thy Grace shall have it. (*He wraps* STEPHANO *with the gown.*)

CALIBAN Do the murder first. If he awake,
He'll fill our skins with pinches,
make us strange stuff.

STEPHANO Be you quiet, monster. Mistress line, is not this my
jerkin?* (*Takes it down*)
Now jerkin, you are like to lose
your hair and prove a bald jerkin.*

TRINCULO Do, do!* We steal by line and level,* and't like* your
grace.

STEPHANO I thank thee for thy jest. Here's a garment for 't. (*Hands
him a garment*)
Wit shall not go unrewarded while I am king
of this country. (*Hands him another*)
Monster, go to, carry this. – (*Hands him more.*)

TRINCULO And this – (*Hands him even more clothing.*)

SPIRITS *are beckoned on by* PROSPERO. *They enter and dance
all around* CALIBAN, STEPHANO *and* TRINCULO. *Eventually*
STEPHANO, CALIBAN *and* TRINCULO *are driven out by the spirits.*

PROSPERO Let them be hunted soundly.

jerkin: kind of jacket   **bald jerkin:** sailors who lose their hair from fever   **do,
do:** fine, fine   **line and level:** plumb line   **and't like:** if it please

Shortly shalt have the air of freedom. For a little
Follow, and do me service.

ARIEL *quickly exits and immediately returns with a magic robe as we segue without pause to the final Act.*

ACT V
SAME PLACE

Enter ARIEL *and places a magician's robe on* PROSPERO.

PROSPERO Now does my project gather to a head.
    How's the day?

ARIEL On the sixth hour, at which time, my lord,
    You said our work should cease.

PROSPERO I did say so
    When first I raised the tempest. Say, my spirit,
    How fares the King and 's followers?

ARIEL Just as you left them, all prisoners, sir,
    They cannot budge till you release. But chiefly
    Him that you termed, sir, the good old Lord Gonzalo,
    His tears run down his beard like winter's drops
    From eaves of reeds.* Your charms so strongly works 'em;
    That if you now beheld them, your affections
    Would become tender.

PROSPERO Dost thou think so, spirit?

ARIEL Mine would, sir, were I human. (*Pause*)

PROSPERO And mine shall. They being penitent,
    The sole drift of thy purpose doth extend
    Not a frown further. Go, release them, Ariel,
    My charms I'll break, their senses I'll restore,
    And they shall be themselves.

ARIEL I'll fetch them, sir.

Exit ARIEL.

reeds: a thatched roof

PROSPERO This rough magic
    I here abjure, and when I have required*
    Some heavenly music (which even now I do)
    To work mine end upon their senses that*
    This airy charm is for, I'll break my staff,
    Bury it certain fathoms in the earth
    And deeper than did ever plummet sound
    I'll drown my book. (*Solemn music*)

Enter ARIEL *while* ALONSO, GONZALO, SEBASTIAN, ANTONIO,
ADRIAN *and* FRANCISCO *follow and stand in a circle unmoving.*
PROSPERO *approaches each and addresses them.*

PROSPERO Holy Gonzalo, honorable man,
    Mine eyes fall fellowly drops* O good Gonzalo,
    My true preserver, I will pay thy graces
    Home* both in word and deed. Most cruelly
    Didst thou, Alonso, use me and my daughter.
    Thou art pinched for 't now, Sebastian. Flesh and blood,
    You, brother mine, that entertained ambition,
    Expelled remorse* and nature;* whom, with Sebastian
    Would here have killed your king, I do forgive thee.
    Ariel, fetch me the hat and rapier in my cell.
    I will discase* me, and myself present
    As I was sometime Milan. Quickly, spirit!
    Thou shalt ere long be free.

ARIEL *removes* PROSPERO's *robe, exits with it and immediately returns
singing and dresses* PROSPERO *in his regal hat and sword.*

ARIEL In a cowslip's bell I lie;
    There I couch when owls do cry.

---

required: asked for **their senses that:** the senses of those whom **drops:** tears
of sympathy **home:** and thy favors **remorse:** pity **nature:** natural feelings
discase: remove my magician's robe

On the bat's back I do fly
Merrily, merrily shall I live now
Under the blossom that hangs on the bough.

PROSPERO Why, that's my dainty Ariel! I shall miss thee,
But yet thou shalt have freedom;
To the king's ship, invisible as thou art!
There shalt thou find the mariners asleep
Under the hatches. The Boatswain
Being awake, enforce them to this place,
And presently,* I prithee.

ARIEL I drink the air before me, and return
Or ere your pulse twice beat.

Exit ARIEL.

GONZALO All torment, trouble, wonder, and amazement
Inhabits here. Some heavenly power guide us
Out of this fearful country!

PROSPERO Behold, sir King,
The wronged Duke of Milan, Prospero,
For more assurance that a living prince
Does now speak to thee, I embrace thy body.
And to thee and thy company I bid
A hearty welcome. (*Embraces him*)

ALONSO Whe'r* thou be'st he or no,
Th' affliction of my mind amends, with which,
I fear, a madness held me. This must crave*
(And if this be at all)* a most strange story. (*He kneels.*)
Thy dukedom I resign and do entreat

---

presently: immediately   **whe'r:** whether   **crave:** require   (**And if this be at all**): if this is really happening

Thou pardon me my wrongs. But how should Prospero
Be living and be here?

PROSPERO (*Lifts him up*) First, noble friend,
Let me embrace thine age, whose honor cannot
Be measured or confined.

GONZALO Whether this be
Or be not, I'll not swear.

PROSPERO (*To* GONZALO) you do yet taste
Some subtleties* o' th' isle, that will not let you
Believe things certain. Welcome, my friends all.
(*Aside to* SEBASTIAN *and* ANTONIO)
But you, my brace of lords were I so minded,
I here could pluck his Highness' frown upon you,
And justify* you traitors. At this time
I will tell no tales.

SEBASTIAN (*Aside*) The devil speaks to him.

PROSPERO No.
For you, most wicked sir, whom to call brother
I do forgive thy rankest fault – all of them; and require
My dukedom of thee, which perforce I know
Thou must restore.

SEBASTIAN *and* ANTONIO *move to another part of the stage.*

ALONSO If thou beest Prospero,
Give us particulars of thy preservation;
How thou hast met us here, whom three hours since
Were wracked upon this shore; where I have lost
My dear son Ferdinand.

PROSPERO I am woe* for 't, sir.

subtleties: deception   **justify:** prove   **woe:** sorry

ALONSO Irreparable is the loss, and patience
    Says it is past her cure.

PROSPERO I rather think
    You have not sought her help, of whose soft grace
    And rest myself content.

ALONSO You the like loss?

PROSPERO As great to me, at late,* for I have lost my daughter.

ALONSO A daughter?
    O heavens, that they were living both in Naples,
    The King and Queen there! That they were, I wish
    Myself were mudded in that oozy bed
    Where my son lies. When did you lose your daughter?

PROSPERO In this last tempest. (*Addresses* ALL)
    Know for certain that I am Prospero, and that very duke
    Which was thrust forth of Milan, who most strangely
    Upon this shore, where you were wracked, was landed
    To be the lord on 't. No more yet of this;
    My dukedom since you have given me again,
    I will requite you with as good a thing,
    At least bring forth a wonder to content ye
    As much as me my dukedom.

Enter FERDINAND *and* MIRANDA.

ALONSO If this prove
    A vision of the island, one dear son
    Shall I twice love.

SEBASTIAN A most high miracle!

at late: as your loss

FERDINAND Though the seas threaten, they are merciful.
   I have cursed them without cause. (*Kneels*)

ALONSO Now all the blessings
   Of a glad father compass thee about!
   Arise, and say how thou cam'st here. (FERDINAND *rises.*)

MIRANDA O, wonder!
   How many goodly creatures are there here!
   How beauteous mankind is! O brave new world
   That has such people in 't!

PROSPERO 'Tis new to thee.

ALONSO What is this maid?
   Your eld'st* acquaintance cannot be three hours.
   Is she the goddess that hath severed us
   And brought us thus together?

FERDINAND Sir, she is mortal;
   But by immortal providence she's mine.
   I chose her when I could not ask my father
   For his advice, nor thought I had one. She
   Is daughter to this famous Duke of Milan.
   But never saw before; of whom I have
   Received a second life; and second father
   This lady makes him to me.

GONZALO I have inly wept,
   Or should have spoken ere this. Look down, you gods,
   And on this couple drop a blessèd crown.

ALONSO (*To* FERDINAND *and* MIRANDA) Give me your hands.
   Let grief and sorrow still* embrace his heart
   That doth not wish you joy.

---

eld'st: longest   **still:** forever

GONZALO Be it so! Amen!

ALONSO These are not natural events; they strengthen
From strange to stranger.
Say, how came you hither?
Some oracle must rectify our knowledge.

PROSPERO Sir, my liege,
Do not infest your mind with beating on
The strangeness of this business. At picked leisure,
Which shall be shortly, single I'll resolve you
Of every these happened accidents.*
(*Aside to* ARIEL) Set Caliban and his companion free.
Untie the spell.

Exit ARIEL.

How fares my gracious sir?
There are yet missing of your company
Some few odd lads that you remember not.

Enter ARIEL; *driving in* CALIBAN, STEPHANO *and* TRINCULO
wearing their stolen apparel and, yes, they are still drunk.

STEPHANO Every man shift for all the rest, and let no man
take care for himself; for all is but fortune.

CALIBAN How fine my master is! I am afraid
He will chastise me.

PROSPERO These three have robbed me, and this demi-devil
Had plotted with them
To take my life. Two of these fellows you
Must know and own; this thing of darkness I
Acknowledge mine.

accidents: incidents

CALIBAN (*Sits, removing his stolen cloak.*) I shall be pinched to death.

ALONSO Is not this Stephano, my drunken butler?

STEPHANO O, touch me not! (*Quickly throws his stolen robe back over himself.*)
I am not Stephano, but a cramp.

ALONSO This is a strange thing as e'er I looked on.

PROSPERO He is as disproportioned in his manners
As in his shape. Go, sirrah, to my cell;
Take with you your companions. As you look
To have my pardon, trim it handsomely.

CALIBAN (*Rises*) Ay, that I will; and I'll be wiser hereafter,
And seek for grace.

PROSPERO Go to! Away!

(*Exit CALIBAN, STEPHANO and TRINCULO.*)

PROSPERO Sir, I invite your highness and your train
To my poor cell, where you shall take your rest
For this one night, with such discourse
The story of my life, and in the morn
I'll bring you to your ship, and so to Naples,
Where I have hope to see the nuptial
Of these our dear belovèd solemnized.

ALONSO I long
To hear the story of your life, which must
Take* the ear strangely. (*He nods in reverence to PROSPERO as ALL but ARIEL and PROSPERO exit.*)

PROSPERO My Ariel, chick,*

take: captivate   **chick:** term of endearment or i.e., a bird seeking freedom

That is thy charge. Then to the elements
Be free, and fare thou well!

ARIEL *looks for confirmation as* PROSPERO *reaches out to shake*
ARIEL's *hand.* * ARIEL *slowly reaches and shakes* PROSPERO's *hand.*
ARIEL *then turns and walks out (possibly as a man).*

shake Ariel's hand: This direction does not come from Shakespeare but simply
a concept for your consideration.

EPILOGUE

Spoken by PROSPERO *directly to the audience.*

Now my charms are all o'erthrown,
    And what strength I have's mine own.
    Let me not,
    Since I have my dukedom got
    And pardoned the deceiver, dwell
    In this bare island by your spell;
    But Release me from my bands*
    With the help of your good hands.*
    Now I want*
    Spirits to enforce, art to enchant;
    And my ending is despair
    Unless I be relieved by prayer,*
    Which pierces so that it assaults
    Mercy itself and frees all faults.
    As you from crimes would pardoned be,
    Let your indulgence set me free.

PROSPERO *nods respectfully to the audience, turns and exits.*

FINIS

my bands: bonds   **good hands:** an applause to break the spell   **want:** lack
prayer: this petition

ABOUT THE AUTHOR

Cass Foster, Author

Cass Foster, professor emeritus of theatre, has been actively involved in the theatre as an educator, director, fight choreographer and playwright.

His teaching experience includes The Ohio State University, Otterbein College, Central Arizona Central Arizona College, and Mesa Community College. He has directed productions or choreographed fights at Oceanside Productions, Players Theatre Columbus, University of Illinois: Champaign-Urbana, Phoenix Theatre, Arizona State University, Northern Arizona University, the Grand Canyon Shakespeare Festival, Case Western Reserve University, Arizona Jewish Theatre, and the Lyric Opera Theatre of Arizona State University.

Foster is equally known for his groundbreaking *Sixty-Minute Shakespeare* series, which makes the Bard's work accessible to those who lack the time to tackle the unabridged versions of the world's most widely read playwright. The series includes *A Midsummer Night's Dream, Hamlet, Macbeth, Much Ado About Nothing, Romeo and Juliet, Taming of the Shrew, Twelfth Night* and his newest book, *The Tempest.* The *Sixty-Minute Shakespeare* series can be found in all fifty US states, all Canadian provinces, and in forty-five countries. countries. Foster is also the author of *Shakespeare for Children: The Story of Romeo and Juliet,* and he co-authored *To Teach or Not to Teach: Teaching Shakespeare Made Fun!* with Lynn G. Johnson.

Foster resides on the beautiful Hawaiian island of Kauai, with his wife, Nellie, and their dog, Maximus.

ABOUT THE PUBLISHER

Linda F. Radke, President

Linda F. Radke, veteran publisher and owner of Five Star Publications, Inc. has been ahead of her game since 1985, producing and marketing award-winning books for adults and children worldwide. Self-publishing before it was commonplace, setting the bar for partnership publishing and professionally fulfilling traditional publishing contracts, Radke has established Five Star Publications, Inc. as an industry leader in creativity, innovation and customer service.

Five Star Publications, Inc. is proud of its reputation for excellence, producing premium quality books for clients and authors, successfully navigating each stage of the publishing process. Many Five Star titles have been recognized on local, national, and international levels, and their authors have enjoyed promotional opportunities in schools, corporations, and media venues. Recent honors include: National Books Festival Kids & Teachers Resources 52 Great Reads selections; ONEBOOKAZ for Kids; Southwest Books of the Year; One Book, One Community designations; Moonbeam Children's Book Awards; and numerous Glyph, London Book Festival, and Paris Book Festival awards.

Herself an acclaimed writer, Radke is the author of *The Economical Guide to Self-Publishing* and *Promote Like a Pro: Small Budget, Big Show*. Association, Linda also was named "Book Marketer of the Year" by Book Publicists of Southern California and has received numerous public relations and marketing awards.

Having assembled a team of dozens of skilled industry professionals, Radke is committed to helping both established and aspiring authors of all ages continually reach new heights.

The introduction to SHAKESPEARE is not an easy task.
Sometimes the magic can use a little assistance...

Don't Miss These Bestselling Books!

To make the works of Shakespeare accessible to all ages and
levels of education, Cass Foster combines his experience as a
professor emeritus of theatre, fight choreographer and stage
director to provide *Shakespeare: To Teach or not to Teach*,
Shakespeare for Children, and the *Sixty-Minute Shakespeare*
series—judiciously condensed versions of the Bard's classics.
Titles sold individually or as a set.